My Science Library

Who Do I Look Like?

A Book about Animal Babies

by Julie K. Lundgren

Science Content Editor:
Kristi Lew

Rourke
Educational Media

rourkeeducationalmedia.com

Science content editor: Kristi Lew
A former high school teacher with a background in biochemistry and more than 10 years of experience in cytogenetic laboratories, Kristi Lew specializes in taking complex scientific information and making it fun and interesting for scientists and non-scientists alike. She is the author of more than 20 science books for children and teachers.

www.rourkeeducationalmedia.com

Photo credits:
Cover © Sari ONeal, Peter Wollinga, Lars Christensen, Utekhina Anna; Cover logo frog © Eric Pohl, test tube © Sergey Lazarev; Page 3 © Becky Sheridan; Page 4/5 © Donna Beeler; Page 6/7 © Ron Rowan Photography; Page 8/9 © Sari ONeal; Page 10/11 © Utekhina Anna; Page 12/13 © Kokhanchikov; Page 14/15 © knin; Page 16/17 © Mircea Bezergheanu; Page 18-21 © Emajy Smith; Page 22 © Ron Rowan Photography, Emajy Smith, Utekhina Anna; Page 23 © Emajy Smith, Becky Sheridan, knin

Editor: Kelli Hicks

Cover and page design/layout by Nicola Stratford, bdpublishing.com

Library of Congress Cataloging-in-Publication Data

Lundgren, Julie K.
 Who do i look like? : a book about animal babies / Julie K. lundgren.
    p. cm. -- (My science library)
 ISBN 978-1-61741-719-1 (Hard cover)
 ISBN 978-1-61741-921-8 (Soft cover)
 1. Animals--Infancy--Juvenile literature. I. Title.
 QL763.L856 2012
 591.3'9--dc22
                                      2011003754

Rourke Educational Media
Printed in the United States of America,
North Mankato, Minnesota

rourkeeducationalmedia.com

customerservice@rourkeeducationalmedia.com   •   PO Box 643328 Vero Beach, Florida 32964

Look! A baby **raccoon**.

A raccoon looks like its **parents.**

Look! A **caterpillar**.

A caterpillar does not look like its parents.

Butterflies are a caterpillar's parents.

Look! A **kitten**.

A kitten looks like
its parents.

Cats are a kitten's parents.

13

Look! A **tadpole**.

A tadpole does not look like its parents.

Frogs are a tadpole's parents.

17

Look! A **foal**.

A foal looks like
its parents.

1. What animal babies look like their parents?

2. Name two animal babies who do not look like their parents.

3. What are some differences between a caterpillar and its parents?

Picture Glossary

caterpillar (KAT-er-pill-er):
This animal first hatches from an egg and then changes into a moth or butterfly.

foal (FOHL):
A foal is a baby horse. It has long legs, a mane, and a tail just like its parents.

kitten (KIT-uhn):
A kitten is a baby cat. Like its parents, a kitten has fur, four legs, and a meow.

parents (PAIR-uhnts):
Parents are mothers and fathers of animal babies.

raccoon (ra-KOON):
A raccoon is a gray, furry animal with a black mask and striped tail.

tadpole (TAD-pohl):
This animal first hatches from an egg and then becomes a frog or toad.

Index

baby 3

caterpillar(s) 6, 8, 9

foal(s) 18, 20

kitten(s) 10, 12, 13

raccoon 3

tadpole(s) 14, 16, 17

Websites

www.biokids.umich.edu/critters/Anura/

www.dnr.wi.gov/eek/

www.kidsbutterfly.org/life-cycle

About the Author

Julie K. Lundgren grew up near Lake Superior where she liked to muck about in the woods, pick berries, and expand her rock collection. Her interests led her to a degree in biology. She lives in Minnesota with her family.